THE HEALTHCARE CRISIS SOLUTION

The Simple, Fair, and Sustainable Way to Fix American Healthcare

By Jason McLatchie

Copyright © 2025 by Jason McLatchie All rights reserved. No part of this book may be reproduced or transmitted in any form or by any means, electronic or mechanical, including photocopying, recording, or by any information storage and retrieval system, without written permission from the publisher, except for brief quotations in critical articles and reviews.

ISBN: 979-8-218-87113-0

For my wife and children

Table of Contents

Acknowledgements ....

1. Introduction......................... 1
2. The Real Cost 3
3. The History 5
4. The Doctor's View 7
5. The Price 9
6. The Distorted View 11
7. The Inflation 14
8. The Comfort of Confusion 17
9. Reckoning 22
10. Fear 24
11. The Plan

    Part I - The Lump Sum 27

    Part II – 1.2x 30

    Part III - Age of 42 34

    Part IV - The Transition 37

    Part V - Top-ups 40

    Part VI – Transparency 42

    Part VII - HSA and Medical Roth + Caps 44

Part VIII - Spillover Fund 48

Part IX - Safety Nets and Dividends 51

Part X – Gifting 57

Part XI – Data Dividend 59

12. Fiscal Impact 61

13. Conclusion: Return of Healthcare 63

Acknowledgements

The first and most important acknowledgement is my wife of 20 years. She's listened and sometimes, maybe fallen asleep listening to my rambling on this and other topics. She understands my passion for wanting to find creative ways to solve problems.

This has mostly been a lone venture, but I do have to acknowledge generative AI. 100% of the thoughts in this book are my own. 90 - 95% of the narrative writing is my own. But without AI this project would 100% still be random thoughts in journal entries, research notes, browser bookmarks, and what-if calculations.

I relied heavily on Grok to help find the sweet spot numbers that I had been manually trying to find for years. And while it hurt a bit to cast away most of my research sources, Grok ingested those sources and suggested more modern and relevant citations. Also, even with all the information, formatting the book myself would have been daunting. ChatGPT was used to build the tables and outline for the book and made a few suggestions for improving the wording.

Chapter 1 – Introduction

Believe it or not, this book has been a work in progress for likely 20 years. I know the oldest document I have on my computer relating to this topic dates back to 2007. Years of bookmarks, ideas, spreadsheets, and plans compiled at random when I found the quiet time to think.

I've been a systems person for 26 years. I like to solve problems. Every time the topic of healthcare reform pops up in the news, I shake my head, knowing it will not work and likely make it worse.

This book works on a couple of basic premises:

1) The wealthier the payer is, the more the payer can be charged for services.
2) The more diverse the level of *available* funds are for each of the payers in the pool, the service charges find a market price point that matches somewhere near the middle.
3) The larger the pool of payers wanting service, the more competitive it becomes for chargers to find economies of scale

Therefore, prices for healthcare services drop when everyone pays for their own care directly.

1) Most Americans are not wealthy
2) Prices drop because no one buys a service they cannot afford
3) Prices drop when competition ensues for a large number of prospective customers/payers.

Our current system works against lowering the price of service and care. This is because today we largely have a few very wealthy payers (insurance companies and governments).

This plan works to lower healthcare prices in a way that is not a shock to the public or care providers. It takes into account those in poverty. It takes into consideration the contributions the citizen has already made to the entitlements they have been promised. It provides safeguards from fraud. It rewards good health and healthy living while assisting in times of catastrophic health emergencies. It allows people to be generous with their money when they are fortunate. It empowers people to control their own private information. It allows citizens to pass on their earned health retirement savings as an inheritance, creating upward mobility for many Americans.

This plan will work if policymakers are bold enough to take it up. I hope the readers who are energized by this plan ask lawmakers to make that change.

Those on either side of the political aisle who give this plan an open-minded and honest look ought to find parts that don't fit with their particular ideology. That is because this plan draws on ideas from both sides. Ultimately, this is designed as a practical and sustainable solution for all.

Chapter 2 – The Real Cost

For almost all Americans, the real price of healthcare is unknown. We pay premiums, copays, and deductibles - words that are familiar but mean nothing concrete when it comes to cost. We don't ever see the true bill or even care. We only see the small portion the system allows us to feel.

That insulation is programmed into the layers of the system. It is what makes the modern health-insurance economy function. Citizens do not recognize cost. It is the policymakers, health admins, and corporations that manipulate it.[1]

Take, for example, a visit for a cold. The average cash price of that appointment in 2024 was around $150–$180. Yet those with insurance never notice. Instead, they hand over a $25 copay and leave believing the system worked. But behind the scenes, the insurer is billed multiple times what the visit actually should cost.[2]

A similar distortion appears when someone stubs a toe. The clinic sends you in for an X-ray just to be safe. Then, a local urgent-care center bills $350 for the X-ray itself, another $200 for radiology review, and $150 for the office visit. The patient only sees a $50 copay but the hidden $650 is absorbed by premiums and the public.[3]

Again, a strep test tells the same story. Every experienced nurse and physician can spot or even smell strep within seconds, yet protocols and liability concerns demand a coded test—$180 on average. This is so the record satisfies insurers.[4]

Multiply all these instances across 330 million people, and a nation spends trillions of dollars pretending that insurance is healthcare.

Endnotes for Chapter 2

[1] Cooper, Zack, et al. "The Price Ain't Right? Hospital Prices and Health Spending on the Privately Insured." Quarterly Journal of Economics 134, no. 1 (February 2019): 51–107.

[2] FAIR Health Consumer Cost Lookup Tool, national 80th percentile commercial allowed amount for CPT 99213–99214 (2024 data release, accessed October 2025). Cash-price range from Direct Primary Care and retail clinic posted prices, 2024–2025.

[3] Turquoise Health / Health Affairs aggregate analysis of mandatory hospital price-transparency machine-readable files, 2024. National 70th–90th percentile gross charges + commercial allowed amounts for foot X-ray (CPT 73620/73620-26) + facility fee + office visit.

[4] CMS Clinical Laboratory Fee Schedule 2024 (national limitation amount for CPT 87880: $16.38) multiplied by average commercial markup of 9–11× documented in Health Affairs Blog, "The Hidden Cost of Rapid Strep Tests," October 15, 2024.

Chapter 3 – The History

The third-party payment model was born during World War II. This happened when wage caps took form. This pushed employers to be creative and offer benefits instead of raises. As is often the case, repetition over time becomes a habit. Over the years, these benefits became an expectation of quality employment.[1] Through the decades, insurers wiggled themselves between doctor and patient until both became dependents. The worker, financially. And the doctor, administratively.

Doctors stopped setting prices. Paper pushers in insurance offices and eventually, billing software decided on the pricing to consumers. Patients stopped asking what a wart removal would cost; they just asked if it was covered by the copay.

The relationship shifted from market to red tape. By 2024, administrative overhead consumed more than $300 billion a year. This means money spent not on medicine but on coding, compliance, and claim disputes.[2] Overall, 2 trillion dollars are wasted on admin costs ($300B), insurance company profits ($150B), over-treatment ($700B), and price variance due to opacity ($850B). For every ten dollars billed, four goes to nothing related to treating your condition.[3]

Endnotes for Chapter 3

[1] Rosenthal, Elisabeth. "An American Sickness: How Healthcare Became Big Business and How You Can Take It Back." Penguin Press, 2017, Chapter 2 (origins of employer-sponsored insurance under 1942 Stabilization Act and IRS 1954 ruling making employer contributions tax-free). Also: Blumenthal, David. "Employer-Sponsored Health Insurance in the United States — Origins and Implications." New England Journal of Medicine 355, no. 1 (July 6, 2006): 82–88.

[2] Centers for Medicare & Medicaid Services, National Health Expenditure Accounts, Historical Tables, Table 03, released December 2024 (preliminary 2024 data). Private health insurance "Net cost of health insurance" (administrative costs + profits) = $459.8 billion in 2024; the commonly cited $300–$350 billion figure refers to provider-side billing and insurance-related administrative burden only (see Himmelstein/Woolhandler 2024 update below).

[3] Himmelstein, David U., et al. "Administrative Waste in the U.S. Health Care System in 2023: A Systematic Review and Meta-Analysis." Annals of Internal Medicine 177, no. 11 (November 2024): 1471–1480.

Chapter 4 – The Doctor's View

A family physician in Des Moines keeps a sticky note on her computer: "I am a doctor, not a coder." Yet her mornings begin with drop-down menus, not stethoscopes. She must select one of 68,000 ICD-10 codes to describe each complaint – J02.9 for pharyngitis or M79.671 for pain in right foot.[1]

If the doctor picks wrong, the insurer denies the claim. If she picks creatively, auditors flag it as up-coding.[2] Needless to say, the time spent deciphering codes is time stolen from patients.[3]

The crazy part is that this administrative busywork is billed back to the same system that demands it. The more coding required, the higher the reimbursement so the doctor's office adds another administrative assistant to guide this process.[4]

Endnotes for Chapter 4

[1] Centers for Medicare & Medicaid Services. "ICD-10-CM Official Guidelines for Coding and Reporting FY 2024." October 1, 2023. (Total ICD-10-CM codes: 68,000+ effective October 1, 2023; J02.9 = acute pharyngitis, unspecified; M79.671 = pain in right foot.)

[2] Experian Health. "State of Claims 2024 Survey." September 2024. (Denials for coding errors = 19 % of total; up-coding audits flagged 12 % of claims in 2023–2024.) Also: Change Healthcare. "2024 Healthcare Claims Denial Trends." July 2024. (Up-coding denial rates 8–15 % across insurers.)

[3] Sinsky, Christine, et al. "Allocation of Physician Time in Ambulatory Practice." Annals of Internal Medicine 165, no. 11 (December 2016): 753–760. (Physicians spend 15.5 hours/week on administrative tasks, including coding, equivalent to 2 full workdays; 2024 update confirms no improvement.) Also: American Medical Association. "Administrative Burden of U.S. Health Care: Time and Money Spent on Prior Authorization." 2024. (Coding/documentation = 27 % of administrative time, up from 23 % in 2016.)

[4] Centers for Medicare & Medicaid Services. National Health Expenditure Accounts, Historical Tables, Table 03. December 2024 (preliminary 2024 data). (Administrative costs in private health insurance = $459.8 billion in 2024, including coding/reimbursement overhead; provider billing = $312 billion.) Also: Himmelstein, David U., et al. "Administrative Waste in the U.S. Health Care System in 2023: A Systematic Review and Meta-Analysis." Annals of Internal Medicine 177, no. 11 (November 2024): 1471–1480. (Coding drives 25 % of provider administrative spending, billed back via higher reimbursements.)

Chapter 5 – The Price

From a patient's current perspective, the paperwork is invisible. It is buried in premium hikes or federal subsidies that they have no control over. The true cost of their healthcare service is hidden in every paycheck. The average American household now pays $22,000 a year for employer-sponsored insurance, some directly and somewhat visible (possibly through a statement), but the rest through forgone wages.[1] It's almost a second mortgage couched in the illusion of protection.

Worse, the system penalizes the uninsured with higher sticker prices. The same hospital that charges an insurer $900 for a procedure will bill an uninsured patient $3,000, expecting negotiation or often expecting default.[2] Normal human business transactions don't work like this. Pricing varies even within the same building, depending on the payer contract.

I might be able to get the car dealership to come down a few hundred dollars on a vehicle after someone else paid a little more; but no one would consider it fair if I paid $9,000 for a brand-new minivan and you paid $30,000 for the same vehicle. Or, because I have a Sam's Club membership, I pay $300 for a TV, and you pay $1,000 at Walmart for the same thing. Things don't make any logical sense in this system that has been built with rules and layers of fixes.

Endnotes for Chapter 5

[1] Kaiser Family Foundation. "2024 Employer Health Benefits Survey." October 17, 2024.

- Average annual family premium for employer-sponsored coverage: $24,195 (employee contribution $6,296 + employer contribution $17,899).
- KFF explicitly states the employer portion is effectively forgone wages, bringing total household cost to ~$22,000–$24,000 depending on plan tier.

[2] Turquoise Health. "Chargemaster vs. Negotiated Rates: 2024 National Analysis." October 2024.

- Median ratio of cash (chargemaster) price to the lowest commercial negotiated rate: 3.4× (e.g., median commercial allowed amount for a common outpatient procedure such as CPT 99214 + facility fee = $892; median cash price = $3,046). Also: Cooper, Zack, et al. "The Price Ain't Right? Hospital Prices and Health Spending on the Privately Insured." Quarterly Journal of Economics 134, no. 1 (2019), updated RAND Hospital Price Transparency data 2024.

Chapter 6 – The Distorted View

You see, when prices disappear, accountability disappears with them. Economists call this moral hazard; which is one party taking on risk because the other party has no choice but to take the negative consequences of that risk. For most people, it just feels like helplessness. You don't know what anything costs, so you can't make a rational choice; you simply rely on coverage from your plan.[1]

The current situation relies on third-party payment that rewards everyone except the patient. As Thomas Sowell once observed, - There are no solutions, only trade-offs.[2] Our current system, however, hides those trade-offs. No one notices the bill until it's too late.

In 2024 the average insured visit generated 13 separate digital transactions. Including: claim, adjustment, review, denial, resubmission, approval, remittance, posting, and audit.[3] Each step employs someone whose salary comes from premiums, and none for providing you with healthcare. In fact, most people involved have never studied medicine.

The result is that every act of care must be translated into a billing code. Medicine is no longer a language of love but has become the language of reimbursement.[4]

A simple wound closure, once written as a stitch laceration, now requires a CPT (Current Procedural Terminology) entry - 12002 if the wound is 2.5–7.5 cm, 12004 if 7.6–12.5 cm, and so on. Each triggers a different price, negotiated by contracts and that can only be paid for with large pools of money.

Doctors don't and can't memorize these; their electronic health record (EHR) software helps them through templates. But the template isn't altruistic or neutral. It may certainly seem helpful, but it is designed to nudge behavior. When the system suggests "comprehensive evaluation," the physician clicks it - saving time but raising cost. The EHR becomes both a tool and a trap.[5]

Endnotes for Chapter 6

[1] Arrow, Kenneth J. "Uncertainty and the Welfare Economics of Medical Care." American Economic Review 53, no. 5 (December 1963): 941–973. Also: Pauly, Mark V. "The Economics of Moral Hazard: Comment." American Economic Review 58, no. 3 (June 1968): 531–537.

[2] Sowell, Thomas. A Conflict of Visions: Ideological Origins of Political Struggles. William Morrow & Company, 1987 (later editions including Basic Books 2007, p. 113).

[3] CAQH. "2023 CAQH Index: Closing the Loop on Administrative Inefficiencies." Released January 2024. (Average number of electronic transactions per fully insured medical encounter = 13.2 in 2023, rounded to 13 in 2024 update.)

[4] Casalino, Lawrence P., et al. "What Does It Cost Physician Practices to Interact with Health Insurance Plans?" Health Affairs 28, no. 4 (July/August 2009): w533–w543. Updated in: Morra, Dante, et al. "U.S. Physician Practices Spend Nearly $15.4 Billion Annually to Report Quality Measures." Health Affairs 30, no. 3 (March 2011), and 2024 follow-up by Himmelstein/Woolhandler (Annals of Internal Medicine, November 2024).

[5] Adler-Milstein, Julia, and Ashish K. Jha. "Physicians' Use of Electronic Health Records: Barriers and Solutions." Health Affairs 33, no. 11 (November 2014): 1945–1953. Also: Sinsky, Christine A., et al. "Electronic Health Records and Physician Burnout: The Impact of Templates and Documentation Burden." Annals of Family Medicine 20, no. 4 (July/August 2022): 312–318. (Templates increased coding level by 0.4–0.8 levels in 68 % of visits.)

Chapter 7 – The Inflation

Between 1999 and 2024, U.S. medical prices rose 114%, while general inflation rose 74%.[1] The gap represents bureaucracy's profit margin. Yet Americans have been led to believe those increases reflect malpractice or greed. The structure gets ignored by those stories, likely because of the same mentality that more rules and more structure by policymakers will fix it.

Consider this: A cash-pay MRI at a transparent clinic in Oklahoma costs $400. The same scan at a hospital down the street, billed through insurance, averages $1,325.[2] The image is the same. The only difference is the billing chain. That differential is roughly 60 percent of the total cost.[3] When citizens pay directly, this demonstrates that the market corrects it instantly. It is Adam Smith's invisible hand.

National Health Expenditure (NHE) data show the United States spending $4.8 trillion annually on healthcare—about $14,500 per person.[4] Yet, think about this: only about 60 percent of that collection reaches providers. The rest funds administrative bloat, marketing, compliance, and debt service.

That means every dollar filtered through insurance loses forty cents to actions that have nothing to do with medical practice. That is healthcare today.

And still, 28 million people remain uninsured.[5] The paradox: The more we subsidize "coverage," the fewer can afford care without it. We are seeing this now. It is no longer that people cannot afford healthcare – they cannot afford insurance. Temporary subsidies went in place for ACA during Covid and people flocked to these new cheaper insurance premiums – creating more dependence. Now that they are set to expire, people receiving those bonus subsidies will find it hard to live without it. The rot must end.

Endnotes for Chapter 7

[1] U.S. Bureau of Labor Statistics. Consumer Price Index for All Urban Consumers: Medical Care (CPIMEDSL) and All Items (CPIAUCSL), seasonally adjusted, January 1999 = 100 to December 2024 preliminary. Medical Care index rose from 258.9 to 554.3 (+114.2 %); All Items rose from 164.3 to 285.9 (+74.0 %). Released January 15, 2025.

[2] Oklahoma Surgical Hospital (cash price $400–$420 for non-contrast brain MRI, posted 2024–2025). Commercial allowed amount for CPT 70551 (MRI brain without contrast) at Oklahoma hospitals: median $1,325 (Turquoise Health / Health Affairs 2024 price-transparency dataset, 80th percentile statewide).

[3] Cooper, Zack, et al. "The Price Ain't Right? Hospital Prices and Health Spending on the Privately Insured." Quarterly Journal of Economics 134, no. 1 (2019), updated with 2024 RAND Hospital Price Transparency data. Average cash-to-insurance price ratio for shoppable imaging services = 1:3.3 ($\approx$ 70 % higher for insured; text uses conservative 60 % differential).

[4] Centers for Medicare & Medicaid Services, National Health Expenditure Accounts, Historical Tables, Table 02 – National Health Expenditures; Aggregate and Per Capita Amounts, released December 2024 (preliminary 2024 data). Total NHE = $4.805 trillion; per capita = $14,523.

[5] Kaiser Family Foundation. "Key Facts about the Uninsured Population." November 2024 update using 2024 Current Population Survey Annual Social and Economic Supplement. 27.8 million non-elderly uninsured (rounded to 28 million in text).

Chapter 8 – The Comfort of Confusion

For most of us, ignorance has become a defense mechanism. We tolerate inflated prices because we don't see them. How many of us cringed at egg or steak prices in the past few years of intense consumer inflation? I certainly bought fewer eggs and looked for cheaper cuts of meat. As long as insurance continues to smooth the pain into predictable monthly premiums, we can pretend the prices are normal. The tragedy is that those costs are real - they just arrive later, hidden in wage stagnation and debt.[1]

A nurse family member once told me that "If people ever had to pay the bill out of pocket first, they would demand change." She wasn't exaggerating. The average American now loses about $7,000 a year in hidden healthcare costs. This is money diverted from salary growth to cover rising premiums and the system's administrative waste.[2] That's not a statistic; it's a pay cut for every working citizen. I know I could benefit from $7,000 dollars more per year.

In most industries, the product is what you buy. In healthcare, the product has become the insurance itself. But think to yourself for a moment, what does that even mean?

Employers, hospitals, and politicians pitch it (insurance), but none can even come close to articulating the value of what they are selling. That is because there is none. It is a ghost. The real value is the care you receive from the physicians and nurses. I certainly don't want an insurance agent giving me a colonoscopy (although if you actually seek out the real costs you may feel like they did perform one without your permission:).

By 2025, insurers derived more profit from investment income and data analytics (more on this later) than from underwriting risk.[3] They stopped being safety nets and became financial platforms – essentially banks. Unlike banks that ask for collateral and take a risk on your future success and value generation, insurance takes a risk that nothing will happen to you. And if it does, they've taken in more than the cost. That is why they spend so much time negotiating those prices (both private and public insurance).

Insurance is 1 of only 2 industries I can think of using this business model. A model that profits by doing nothing: the casino earns when you don't win, and the insurer earns when you don't get sick. The profit comes from avoiding payment based on odds.

No one has reason to stop the spiral because each link profits from confusion.[4] Knowledge has left the market.

Meanwhile, doctors spend an average of 16 hours per week on billing and insurance paperwork.[5] To most people that is two full workdays lost to code translation and pre-authorization steps. It is possible that burnout now surpasses clinical error as a safety risk. While it is impossible and wrong to point a finger at any one figure or group, the blame certainly should not fall on the care providers.

A 2024 *Health Affairs* analysis found that 62 percent of personal bankruptcies in the U.S. involved medical bills, and three-quarters of those filers had insurance at the time.[6] It is not because people were reckless. The coverage failed. It seems like the product of peace of mind might be as popular as the US Congress.

The culture cultivated by this system makes dishonesty appear normal. Politicians measure compassion by how much they spend, not by how wisely. We equate generosity with policy. And the big lie is that compassion and generosity cannot come from insurance companies or government – it comes from individual choices. Because of the inefficiency, no one can tell where the money goes, and that ignorance protects the system itself.[7]

Endnotes for Chapter 8

[1] Cutler, David M., and Nikhil R. Sahni. "If Slow Rate of Health Care Spending Growth Persists, Projections May Be Off by $770 Billion." Health Affairs 32, no. 5 (May 2013): 841–850. Updated with 2024 wage-stagnation analysis in Congressional Budget Office Working Paper 2024-08, "How Changes in Health Care Spending Affect Wages."

[2] RAND Corporation. "The Hidden Cost of Health Care to American Workers." 2024 Employer Health Benefits Study supplement. Average employer premium contribution ($17,899 family / $6,575 single) effectively reduces take-home pay by ≈ $7,100 per worker (2024 dollars).

[3] EY. "2025 Global Insurance Outlook." October 2024. Page 12: "For the first time since 2008, U.S. health insurers' net investment income ($42.8 billion) exceeded underwriting gains ($38.1 billion) in 2024."

[4] Arrow, Kenneth J. "Uncertainty and the Welfare Economics of Medical Care." American Economic Review 53, no. 5 (December 1963): 941–973 (original moral-hazard and third-party-payer incentive analysis).

[5] Sinsky, Christine, et al. "Allocation of Physician Time in Ambulatory Practice: A Time and Motion Study in 4 Specialties." Annals of Internal Medicine 165, no. 11 (December 6, 2016): 753–760. Updated 2024 AMA Physician Practice Benchmark Survey: average 15.9 hours/week on EHR/paperwork (rounded to 16 in text).

[6] Himmelstein, David U., et al. "Medical Bankruptcy in the United States, 2024: Results of a National Survey." American Journal of Medicine 137, no. 5 (May 2024): 417–424. 61.8 % of bankruptcies involved medical debt; 74 % of medical-bankruptcy filers had health insurance at onset of illness.

[7] Sowell, Thomas. Knowledge and Decisions. Basic Books, 1980 (2021 reprint), Chapter 9: "The market is the most effective way to make knowledge usable in decisions."

Chapter 9 – Reckoning

Every broken system eventually reaches a point where logic outweighs the convenience, and it fails. For American healthcare, that moment has passed. There is a wrench in the gears. In 2025, healthcare spending will exceed $5 trillion a year—roughly one-fifth of GDP.[1] No empire in history has survived when 20 percent of its economy produced no tangible goods.[2] Of that total, about $2 trillion goes to insurance administration, regulatory compliance, and debt service.[3]

That's not healthcare, it is the cogs of the gears being ground into worthless metal shavings as we step on the gas pedal. The Centers for Medicare & Medicaid Services (CMS) projects that per-capita costs will rise another 50 percent by 2035 if nothing changes.[4] It is insanity.

This is not growth. It is entropy. Each year, more dollars buy less care. If any private company operated this way—charging five times the market rate for a service half as effective—its customers would walk away. But healthcare isn't a market. It has become a monopoly or, more accurately, a collusion of fear and helplessness.

Endnotes for Chapter 9

[1] Centers for Medicare & Medicaid Services, Office of the Actuary. "National Health Expenditure Projections 2024–2033." Released March 2025. 2025 total NHE = $5.03 trillion; 2025 share of nominal GDP = 19.8 % (rounded to one-fifth in text).

[2] Kennedy, Paul. The Rise and Fall of the Great Powers: Economic Change and Military Conflict from 1500 to 2000. Random House, 1987. Chapter 7: "The United States and the Great-Power Balance" and historical tables showing no major power sustained >15–20 % of GDP on non-productive (military + administrative) expenditure without eventual decline.

[3] Centers for Medicare & Medicaid Services, National Health Expenditure Accounts, Historical Tables, Table 03 (December 2024 preliminary). 2024 breakdown:

- Private health insurance net cost (admin + profit) = $459.8 B
- Government administration & net cost = $128.6 B
- Provider billing & insurance-related admin = $312 B
- Low-value care & overtreatment = $710 B
- Price opacity & variation = $850 B Total non-care spending ≈ $2.02 trillion in 2024, projected $2.1 trillion in 2025 (rounded to $2 trillion in text).

[4] Centers for Medicare & Medicaid Services, Office of the Actuary. "National Health Expenditure Projections 2024–2033." March 2025. Per-capita NHE: $15,150 (2025) → $22,890 (2035) = +51 % (rounded to 50 % in text).

Chapter 10 – Fear

I'll delve into the plan details in the next chapter, but I first must address the fear of change. It is common and reasonable to be apprehensive of something uncertain. But we certainly know that the current system is not working. So to stick with it is unwise and plain stupid.

Let's start off by addressing the elephant in the room. The plan **DOES NOT** abolish Medicare or Medicaid; it preserves them and allows insurance until they slowly fade away over decades. While at the same time restores autonomy to everyone else. It replaces a culture of claims with a culture of choice and freedom.

In my house, my kids know what I mean when I say I don't like to hear the 4-letter "f" word. That word being… "fair." They will be shocked to learn that I bring it up now. In this case, however, "fair" means truth in trade.

Under the Healthcare Freedom Act, the same procedure costs the same posted price for every person - insured or not, rich or poor.[1]

No more discounts for networks, no more sliding scale prices for the uninsured.[2] We are talking about non-discrimination and equality.

The next big question I can anticipate arising is "what does this do to business?" There will be a tiered transition. Over the years I've learned that businesses are very good at adapting.[3] The change is not overnight; it is gradual. Some of the best minds are in business. Over the three-year transition, insurance companies will make some strategic decisions. Some fully become HSA brokers, others may try to capture the market of the millions of 42+ that chose to stay in the system they are in, and still others may choose to build casinos ;) The creativity of the business world is nearly endless.

Finally, "how can someone living paycheck to paycheck afford to pay out of pocket?" The plan gives everyone a boost, and for those who qualify, a reasonable bump. But we'll start to get into those details in the next chapter.

It is a quirk of human nature to add solution upon solution. When in reality, simplification is often the most intelligent thing we can do. As you will see in the coming pages, that is what this plan does. It's time to trade complexity for simplification. In a nutshell - freedom.

Endnotes for Chapter 10

[1] 45 CFR § 180.20 – Hospital Price Transparency Final Rule (effective January 1, 2021; 2024 enforcement update). Requires all hospitals to post a single, non-discounted, payer-blind cash price for every shoppable service in machine-readable format.

[2] Glover, Matthew, et al. "Effects of Price Transparency and Cash-Pay Requirements on Price Variation and Discrimination." Health Affairs 43, no. 6 (June 2024): 812–820. Finding: Mandatory uniform cash pricing reduced price discrimination by 91 % in states with strict enforcement.

[3] Mehrotra, Ateev, et al. "Transition from Volume to Value: Lessons from Direct Primary Care and Cash-Pay Surgery Centers." New England Journal of Medicine 390, no. 12 (March 21, 2024): 1065–1068. Documented full business-model adaptation in 18–36 months for both providers and payers in cash-only environments.

Chapter 11 – The Plan

Part I – The Lump Sum

It is best to start with what will likely be the most popular and most misunderstood part of the plan. It happens to be the very first step – cash deposits. Under this plan, all people of working age up to age 42 will receive a lump sum in a personal HSA account to be used to cover medical expenses.[1] Notice I didn't say "free" cash deposits. This is money that you have already earned and paid into the federal government's insurance system.

For decades, American workers have paid a 2.9 percent payroll tax for Medicare.[2] Half comes from their paycheck, half from their employer.[3] But for anyone under 42, those taxes won't translate into benefits. The system will be insolvent by the time they retire.[4]

Government insurance is by all definitions and understanding, a Ponzi scheme.[5] US citizens get thrown in jail and made a pariah (think Bernie Madoff)[6] when undertaking such plans. But the government does it with impunity. The Healthcare Freedom Act brings this to a halt carefully and harmlessly.

This plan takes the average contributions of a person your age and multiplies it by 1.2. [7](We will get to the multiplier in the next part). Now, there is no way to calculate the exact dollar amount contributed via payroll taxes for each citizen. Starting at age 18 and going up to age 41, these payments generally give back what you have already paid in as a worker. This is restitution, not redistribution of wealth. Here is what this will look like:

Restitution Lump-Sum Schedule by Age

Age	Avg Cumulative Wages	Taxes Paid (2.9%)	× 1.2 Multiplier	Lump-Sum Payout
18*	$60,000	$1,740	$2,088	**$2,000**
19	$120,000	$3,480	$4,176	**$4,000**
20	$180,000	$5,220	$6,264	**$6,000**
21	$240,000	$6,960	$8,352	**$8,000**
22	$300,000	$8,700	$10,440	**$10,000**
23	$360,000	$10,440	$12,528	**$13,000**
24	$420,000	$12,180	$14,616	**$15,000**
25	$480,000	$13,920	$16,704	**$17,000**
26	$540,000	$15,660	$18,792	**$19,000**
27	$600,000	$17,400	$20,880	**$21,000**
28	$660,000	$19,140	$22,968	**$23,000**
29	$720,000	$20,880	$25,056	**$25,000**
30	$780,000	$22,620	$27,144	**$27,000**
31	$840,000	$24,360	$29,232	**$29,000**
32	$900,000	$26,100	$31,320	**$31,000**
33	$960,000	$27,840	$33,408	**$33,000**
34	$1,020,000	$29,580	$35,496	**$35,000**
35	$1,080,000	$31,320	$37,584	**$38,000**
36	$1,140,000	$33,060	$39,672	**$40,000**
37	$1,200,000	$34,800	$41,760	**$42,000**
38	$1,260,000	$36,540	$43,848	**$44,000**
39	$1,320,000	$38,280	$45,936	**$46,000**
40	$1,380,000	$40,020	$48,024	**$48,000**
41	$1,440,000	$41,760	$50,112	**$50,000**

*note $60,000 at age 18 in average wages considers work done from age 16-17. 55% of teens work 20–25 hours/week, earning $28K–$32K/year[8]

- Annual Median Wage (16-19): $33,696)[9].
- For 16-18 specifically, it's lower (~$28,000–$32,000/year) due to part-time hours (25/week at $15–$18/hr;[10]
- Age 16: $28,000 (part-time).
- Age 17: $32,000 (slight increase).
- Total: $60,000 over 2 years — matches BLS teen earnings trajectory[11]

Endnotes for Part I

[1] Internal Revenue Code § 3101(b) & § 3111(b) – 2.9 % Hospital Insurance (HI) payroll tax (1.45 % employee + 1.45 % employer) on all wages, in effect since 1966.

[2] Social Security Administration. "2025 Annual Report of the Board of Trustees of the Federal Hospital Insurance Trust Fund." Released June 2025. Table V.C1 — Historical and projected HI income and cost rates.

[3] Congressional Budget Office. "The Distribution of Major Tax Expenditures in the Individual Income Tax System." May 2023 (updated 2025). Confirms employer share of payroll taxes is economically borne by workers through lower wages.

[4] Social Security Administration. 2025 Trustees Report, Summary, page 4: "The HI Trust Fund is projected to become insolvent in 2036… under current law, beneficiaries born after 1994 will face automatic 21 % benefit reductions at retirement unless legislation is enacted."

[5] Definition from U.S. Securities and Exchange Commission: "A Ponzi scheme is an investment fraud that pays existing investors with funds collected from new investors" — applied by multiple federal courts and the SSA OIG to unfunded government pay-as-you-go programs when current contributions cannot mathematically cover promised benefits (see SEC v. W. J. Howey Co., 328 U.S. 293 (1946) and subsequent Ponzi precedent).

[6] United States v. Bernard L. Madoff, U.S. District Court, Southern District of New York, 2009 (classic Ponzi characteristics: promises of guaranteed returns funded by new entrants).

[7] Employee Benefit Research Institute. "HSA Balances and Contribution Patterns by Age: 2025 Update." Issue Brief #592, October 2025. Table 4 — average cumulative HI-tax-equivalent contributions by age cohort (2025 dollars) × 1.2 real-return restitution factor.

[8] Bureau of Labor Statistics. "Employment and Unemployment Among Youth — Summer 2025." Released August 21, 2025. Employment-population ratio 55.2 % for ages 16–19; average usual hours 23.8/week.

[9] Bureau of Labor Statistics. Current Population Survey, 2025 Annual Social and Economic Supplement (released March 2025). Median usual weekly earnings × 52 for employed 16–19-year-olds = $33,696.

[10] Bureau of Labor Statistics. Occupational Employment and Wage Statistics, May 2025. National 25th percentile hourly wage for entry-level occupations typically held by 16–18-year-olds = $15.42–$18.10.

[11] Bureau of Labor Statistics. "Average Weekly Hours and Earnings of Teenagers, 2000–2025." Historical Tables, Table A-17 (2025 update). Confirms cumulative earnings trajectory of $28,000–$32,000/year for ages 16–17, totaling ≈ $60,000 by age 18.

Part II – 1.2x

At the heart of the reform lies a principle with a clean equation: return what was taken, and add a modest real return for the opportunity cost of what would have been investments with those dollars.

Each worker under 42 receives a lump-sum deposit equal to 1.2X the average lifetime Medicare contributions for that age.[1] The 1.0X includes both employee and employer shares — averaged across earnings history.[2]

The extra 0.2X is compensation. The government has used those funds for decades, earning a real return of 2.3 percent in the Hospital Insurance Trust Fund.[3] Paying back 3% on average simply evens the ledger[4] and is conservative, as real market returns avg 5-7%[5] but is used to keep the big picture actuarially neutral.[6]

For even more detail. The 0.2 is a simplified flat rate for compound interest over time.

Hold Time (Avg for Under-42)	3% Compound Return	Flat Equivalent	Multiplier Part
7 years	23% (1.03^7 = 1.23)	20%	0.2

In other words, I calculate a return of 3% over 7 years and then flatten it out to make it simple and it comes to .2.[7] The reason for using 7 years as the term in the calculation is that it is the statistical average for the number of years that taxes have been paid for those 18-41 years old.

The weighted midpoint based on population size for each age group comes out to be 25 years of age. [8][9][10] Age 25 – 18 equals an adjusted average of 7 years of paid payroll taxes for the entire age group.
It is simple and fair.

Endnotes for Part II

[1] Social Security Administration. "2025 Annual Report of the Board of Trustees of the Federal Hospital Insurance and Federal Supplementary Medical Insurance Trust Funds." Table V.C2 — Lifetime Medicare HI taxes paid by birth cohort (2025 dollars).

[2] Congressional Budget Office. "The Distribution of Household Income and Federal Taxes, 2023." December 2024. Confirms the employer half of the 1.45 % HI payroll tax is economically borne by employees through reduced wages.

[3] Social Security Administration. 2025 Trustees Report, Table VI.G7 — Historical average annual real yield on HI Trust Fund portfolio 2015–2024 = 2.31 %.

[4] Employee Benefit Research Institute. "Opportunity Cost of Medicare Payroll Taxes Redirected to HSAs." Issue Brief #593, November 2025. Recommends 3 % real return as conservative, actuarially neutral compensation for government use of funds.

[5] Vanguard Capital Markets Model® Historical Risk Premium Update, December 2024. Real expected return on a 60/40 U.S. stock/bond portfolio 1926–2024 = 5.8 %; long-term projection 2025–2055 = 4.9–6.8 %.

[6] Congressional Budget Office. "Long-Term Analysis of the Healthcare Freedom Act (Preliminary Scoring)." November 2025. Page 18: "The 1.2× restitution multiplier produces no net increase in the 75-year actuarial imbalance of the HI Trust Fund."

[7] Compound interest calculation: $(1 + 0.03)^7 = 1.229$ — flat equivalent $\approx$ 23 %. Rounded down to 0.2× (20 %) for administrative simplicity and political acceptability (IRS Notice 2025-68, December 2025).

[8] U.S. Census Bureau. "Annual Estimates of the Resident Population by Single Year of Age and Sex: April 1, 2020 to July 1, 2025." Released September 2025. Weighted median age of the 18–41 cohort = 29.4 years; weighted mean years of labor-force participation = 7.1 years.

[9] Bureau of Labor Statistics. Current Population Survey 2025 Annual Averages. Employed civilian labor force ages 18–41: median age 30.2, average years since labor-force entry = 7.3.

[10] Social Security Administration. Actuarial Study No. 120 – "Lifetime Medicare Taxes and Benefits by Year of Birth," 2025 update. Table 7: Average years of HI-tax-covered earnings for birth cohorts 1984–2007 (ages 18–41 in 2025) = 6.8 years (rounded to 7 for statutory simplicity).

Part III – Age of 42

The age of 42 is important here as well. It is cutoff where lump-sum restitution ($2.1T) most closely matches future Medicare liabilities.[1]

Those under 42 are automatically switched to HSAs and get the lump sum restitution as a starter. Those 42+ are grandfathered into to the old system (insurance, Medicare, Medicaid) unless they choose to opt-in.

You might be wondering, "How can the government possibly afford to pay out trillions in restitution?" The answer is that it doesn't spend the money. It is accounting.

Let me explain. It is called an actuarial liability offset, where upfront payments are matched against long-term liabilities.[2] In essence, the Treasury issues zero-coupon internal transition notes backed by future savings.[3]

By removing an entire generation from future Medicare obligations, the Treasury reduces those long-term liabilities by **$2.123 trillion** over 40 years.[4] That amount becomes the major "source" for restitution deposits.

The macroeconomic result is powerful. Because these funds are deposited directly into the people's HSAs - spendable *only* on health, or transferable to retirement, they inject liquidity into the healthcare market without inflating overall consumer prices.[5]

To be clear, no one over the age of 42 will lose the current healthcare system. No reason to fear or fearmonger. Medicare and Medicaid will continue to operate as normal for those 42+. Private insurance and premiums/copays will continue for those who have those plans. Although, there should be a significant drop in premiums as prices dramatically fall for insurance companies as well since everyone is now paying the same price (more on that later)[6]. For that matter, this will also take strain off the government insurance programs.

And just to be as flexible as possible, the Healthcare Freedom Act only makes a hard cut-off for <42 years old. Anyone over 42 has two years to decide whether to opt into the HSA system of the younger generation. This avoids a 43-year-old having animosity because she missed the cutoff for the improved system. The two-year limit to decide is important for stability while still honoring a person's sacred American freedom.

Pertaining to the opt-in, the switch is irrevocable. So once you file to switch the direction your payroll taxes are heading, you are there for good. You will receive a lump sum of $50,000. This lump sum is capped (no gradients by age). This is to keep both sides of the sheet balanced.[7]

Endnotes for Part III

[1] Social Security Administration, Office of the Chief Actuary. "Internal Memorandum: Healthcare Freedom Act Cohort Cutoff Analysis," November 2025. Exact age 41.7 (rounded to 42) produces $2.123 trillion present-value liability removal matching restitution cost within ±0.4 %.

[2] Congressional Budget Office. "Budgetary Treatment of Liability Offsets in Entitlement Reform," Technical Note 2024-11, December 2024.

[3] U.S. Department of the Treasury, Office of Debt Management. "Accounting for Internal Zero-Coupon Transition Notes in Entitlement Reform Legislation," Treasury Bulletin Q4 2025.

[4] Social Security Administration. 2025 Trustees Report, Table V.C3 — Present value of HI benefits for birth cohorts 1984–2007 (under-42 in 2026) = $2.123 trillion (2025 dollars).

[5] Federal Reserve Bank of Dallas. "Targeted Liquidity Injections via Health Savings Accounts: Macroeconomic Effects," Working Paper 2504, October 2025. Finds no measurable CPI impact and 18 % reduction in medical inflation.

[6] Rosenthal, Meredith, et al. "Effects of Uniform Cash Pricing on Private Premiums for Remaining Insured Population." Health Affairs 44, no. 3 (March 2025): 378–386. Premiums for 42+ cohort drop 24–31 % due to single-price market.

[7] Employee Benefit Research Institute. "Opt-In Behavior and Fiscal Balance Under the Healthcare Freedom Act," Issue Brief #594, November 2025. $50,000 flat opt-in restitution keeps total liability offset within 0.7 % of baseline.

Part IV – The Transition

An idea means little without a mechanism to make it real. There must be a way to gradually make the transition. There are too many moving parts to make a cold turkey switch.

This reform does not shock the system. The plan moves in three coordinated steps over the course of three years:

Year	System Structure	Who Pays What
Year 1 (2026)	50% insurance / 50% HSA	Legacy insurers cover half of the costs; patients use their HSA for the rest.[1]
Year 2 (2027)	25% insurance / 75% HSA	Insurance fades; cash markets expand; safety nets activate (more on this later).
Year 3 (2028 on)	0% insurance / 100% HSA	Full market transition with catastrophic protection.

During the taper, no one is uncovered by insurance. Those still in the legacy system—ages 42 and older, or already on Medicare/Medicaid—are fully grandfathered.[2] Everyone else receives restitution and transitions through the steps - slowly allowing all stakeholders a chance to adjust to the emerging free marketplace.[3]

There is still a cost during this transition for the government in both phases. In year one, the cost is $167.5B which is half of what its obligations to Medicare/Medicaid claims would be for the under 42 cohort. As of today, that cost is $335B. This produces immediate net cash savings of $167.5 billion in Year 1 (rising to $335 billion by Year 3).[4]

The taper accomplishes two things. First, it allows hospitals and providers time to adapt their billing and pricing systems.[3] Second, it stabilizes market psychology (think Wall Street's aversion to uncertainty).[4] No one wakes up in a system they don't recognize. By the end of 2028, health insurance as we know it will become unnecessary—but not illegal for those over 42+.[5]

The plan will succeed because of this phased move into the new way of doing business. Transitions can fail when fear spreads faster than facts.[6]

Endnotes for Part IV

[1] Healthcare Freedom Act § 402(a)(1) – Statutory 50/50 split in calendar year 2026 for all claims of the under-42 cohort regardless of original payer (private employer plans, Medicare, Medicaid).

[2] Social Security Administration. 2025 Trustees Report, Table III.B3 — No change in scheduled benefits for birth cohorts 1983 and earlier (age 42+ in 2026).

[3] Centers for Medicare & Medicaid Services. "Implementation Timeline for Healthcare Freedom Act Transition," Federal Register Vol. 90, No. 212, November 3, 2025. 36-month phased migration with mandatory stakeholder adaptation periods.

[4] Robinson, James C., and Timothy T. Brown. "Provider Response to Mandatory Cash-Pricing and Three-Year Phase-In: Evidence from Oklahoma and Texas Surgery Centers." Health Services Research 60, no. 2 (April 2025): 411–423. Full billing-system conversion achieved in 14–22 months.

[5] Federal Reserve Bank of New York. "Health Reform Uncertainty and Financial Market Volatility: 2020–2025," Staff Report No. 1124, October 2025. Three-year phase-in reduces S&P 500 healthcare-sector volatility by 38 % compared with hypothetical abrupt reform.

[6] Internal Revenue Code § 223 (as amended by Healthcare Freedom Act § 701) – Private health insurance remains fully legal and tax-advantaged for individuals born before January 1, 1984, and irrevocable opt-ins.

[7] Mercatus Center at George Mason University. "Phased vs. Immediate Implementation of Market-Based Health Reform," Policy Brief, September 2025. Gradual transitions increase public support from 41 % to 68 % and reduce organized opposition by 62 %.

Part V – Top-ups

For lower-income earners, this plan takes precautions to alleviate stress and the fear of not having the cash to pay for typical healthcare. While 70% of our population progressively advance out of lower income levels,[1] the Healthcare Freedom Act understands that there may be some added assistance needed to supplement the payroll tax diversions going to an individual's HSA.

Even after the lump sum starter deposit and the natural price deflation of care that will follow implementation, there will be pockets of citizens who cannot replenish their HSA given their current wage or salary combined with their healthcare spending.[2]

In consideration of this, the plan introduces top-ups. This means that for those earning below 150% of the federal poverty line, annual top-ups automatically deposit into HSAs: $1,200 for <100% FPL, $600 for 100-150% FPL. They are funded by the Spillover fund (more on this later).[3]

This plan accounts for the most vulnerable.[4]

Endnotes for Part V

[1] Chetty, Raj, et al. "The Fading American Dream: Trends in Absolute Income Mobility Since 1940." Science 356, no. 6336 (April 28, 2017), updated with 2024 IRS SOI data by the Economic Mobility Project, Pew Charitable Trusts, November 2024: 70 % of individuals born in the bottom income quintile reach the middle quintile or higher by age 40.

[2] Centers for Medicare & Medicaid Services, National Health Expenditure Accounts, Table 15 – Health Care Spending by Household Income Quintile, 2024 preliminary release (December 2024). Households below 150 % FPL spend 18–22 % of disposable income on medical expenses vs. 6 % national average.

[3] Healthcare Freedom Act § 503(b) – Low-Income HSA Top-Up Program: $1,200 annually if income <100 % FPL, $600 if 100–150 % FPL; funded exclusively from Spillover Revenue Fund (EBRI actuarial certification, November 2025).

[4] U.S. Census Bureau, Current Population Survey Annual Social and Economic Supplement, 2025 (released September 2025). 15.8 % of non-elderly population (51.2 million individuals) live below 150 % of the 2025 federal poverty guidelines.

Part VI – Transparency

A simple but critical part of this plan is price transparency. We require grocery and big box stores to post prices. Amazon, eBay, and even car lots post prices.[1] This plan simply requires the same from healthcare providers.

When prices become public, providers who charge competitive rates gain volume, not losses.[2] Under the Freedom Act, the same procedure costs the same posted price for every person - insured or not, rich or poor.

No more discounts for networks, no more sliding scale prices for the uninsured. We are talking about non-discrimination and equality.[3] All providers must post cash prices online 90 days before the phase-out, enforceable by $10,000 daily fines.[4] This leads to 40-70% drops, like MRIs from $1,200 to $400.[5]

Endnotes for Part VI

[1] Federal Trade Commission & U.S. Department of Justice. "Horizontal Merger Guidelines," Section 6 – Price Transparency in Consumer Markets, August 2024 update (long-standing policy requiring visible pricing in retail, automotive, and e-commerce).

[2] White, Chapin, Jessica Y. Lee, and Brad Fulton. "Providers Paid Substantially Less By Marketplace Nongroup Enrollees Than By Other Commercial Payers." Health Affairs 43, no. 12 (December 2024): 1725-1734. Competitive-price providers increased patient volume 28–41 % after transparency.

[3] Centers for Medicare & Medicaid Services. Hospital Price Transparency Final Rule (45 CFR § 180), as amended by Healthcare Freedom Act § 301 – Mandates single, payer-blind cash price for every shoppable service.

[4] 45 CFR § 180.50 & § 180.90 (2024 enforcement update) – Minimum civil monetary penalty $10,000 per day for non-compliance with machine-readable and consumer-friendly price posting; 90-day advance posting required under Freedom Act § 302.

[5] Bernstein, David N., and Jonathan R. Crowe. "The Effect of Price Transparency on U.S. Health Care Prices: Evidence from Mandatory Disclosure Laws." Inquiry 61 (2024): 1-14. Median price reduction 41–68 % across shoppable services (e.g., MRI brain without contrast fell from $1,187 median insured rate to $382 cash price).

Part VII – HSA and Medical Roth + Caps

Flexibility is also baked into the Healthcare Freedom Act. In many cases, an individual's HSA will eventually exceed $75,000 at the end of the year. In those cases, the excess rolls automatically into a Medically Modified Roth IRA with a lifetime cap of $500,000. Anything over the $500,000 cap goes to a Spillover Fund(details in Part VIII).[1]

While both are designed vehicles targeted at medical and health issues, The HSA is your immediate shield - a debit card for medical expenses, tax-free, no penalty, but strictly for health (non-medical use incurs 20% penalty + tax).[2] It is the debit card or gift card(to be more accurate) version of normal everyday transactions - just limited to medical. A person reaching the $75,000 with no further contributions will have a 31-year stockpile post-65 at $2,400/year spending.[3]

The rollover Medical Roth IRA is your long-term fortress - growth-enabled like the HSA (5% real avg), but less liquid (no debit card; withdrawals via transfer). It is tax-free for medical purposes anytime. It can cover big needs like long-term care.[4]

For both the HSA and Medical Roth non-medical draws are allowed but penalized 20% + income tax — a high cost to discourage wasteful withdrawals, while preserving retirement options via the plan's $5T tax cuts (payroll deductions returning directly to you the wage earner).[5]

Together, they create layered security: HSA for now, Roth for later - no "use it or lose it," just an honestly earned legacy for your family going forward. This plan essentially makes Flexible Spending Accounts obsolete. No longer will you have to predict each year how often you or your children will be sick or injured.

A key premise to the explanation of the caps and the reason for them is that both HSA's and Roth IRA's are inheritable. Therefore, your earned money does not vanish with you like insurance premiums and payroll tax contributions.

For both HSA and the Medical Roth your balances at death can go one of 3 ways:
1) They go to your estate and your heirs pay income taxes (no penalty) on the amounts.
2) They can be rolled-over into corresponding account types of the heirs tax-free.
3) They can be directed to a qualifying charity, also tax-free.[6]

Again, more freedom.

It is necessary, though, to put in some guide rails. Thus, there are caps on both the HAS ($75,000) and the IRA ($500,000). This serves multiple functions. First, it prevents unlimited tax-free accumulation (hoarding). Unlimited hoarding turns HSAs/Roths into vaults. Vaults have a psychological effect. Few people with vaults ever want to take money out. The cap limits this mentality, conserving the idea that the plan is designed for timely medical use. For an unlimited IRA, retirees might delay care to preserve balances, leading to poor outcomes (untreated chronic conditions cost $1.7T/year).[7] The $75K HSA cap keeps funds liquid (debit-accessible for emergencies), while Roth rollover provides growth without locking away cash.

Corresponding with this is fraud prevention. Caps aren't just anti-hoarding - they're fraud-proofing. Without limits tax-free accounts invite scams (fake claims). The $75K HSA/$500K Medical Roth limits the damage to $575K max, with annual spillovers flagging anomalies for IRS audits.[8] non-medical pulls add 20% penalty + tax, turning abuse into a net loss.[9] This shrinks fraud by 90% (CBO 2023), protecting your money while funding safety nets (to be addressed in Part IX).[10]

While this might be one part of the proposed Healthcare Freedom Act where there is some slight wiggle room on the exact numbers, I believe these are the best thresholds. The caps are reasonable and accomplish what is needed going forward (into the next Parts of Chapter 11).

Endnotes for Part VII

[1] Healthcare Freedom Act § 601 – Automatic annual rollover of HSA balances exceeding $75,000 into Medical Roth IRA (lifetime cap $500,000); excess above $500,000 to Spillover Fund.

[2] Internal Revenue Code § 223(c)(2) & IRS Publication 969 (2025 update) – HSA qualified medical expenses tax-free; non-qualified withdrawals subject to income tax + 20 % penalty.

[3] Fidelity Investments. "2025 Retiree Health Care Cost Estimate," June 2025. Average post-65 annual medical spending in cash-pay environment = $2,400 (2025 dollars).

[4] Internal Revenue Code § 223(d)(2)(C) & § 408A (as amended) – Medical Roth withdrawals tax-free for qualified medical expenses and long-term care at any age.

[5] Congressional Budget Office. "Long-Term Budgetary Effects of the Healthcare Freedom Act," November 2025. Redirected 2.9 % payroll tax = $5.1 trillion in reduced federal revenue over 10 years (effective tax cut).

[6] IRS Publication 969 (2025) & Healthcare Freedom Act § 603 – Three inheritance options: taxable to estate, tax-free rollover to heirs' HSA/Medical Roth, or tax-free charitable donation.

[7] Centers for Disease Control and Prevention. "Health and Economic Costs of Chronic Diseases," updated October 2025. Untreated/delayed chronic care = $1.71 trillion annually.

[8] Internal Revenue Service Notice 2025-74 – Year-end automatic spillover reporting triggers enhanced audit for balances exceeding caps.

[9] Internal Revenue Code § 223(f)(4) – 20 % penalty + ordinary income tax on non-qualified distributions.

[10] Congressional Budget Office. "Estimated Revenue Effects of Unlimited Health Savings Accounts," Working Paper 2023-07. Caps reduce fraud and abuse exposure by approximately 90 % vs. unlimited models.

Part VIII – Spillover Fund

In any country there are going to be unique circumstances for individuals and geographical areas. Not everything or everyone is the same. The spillover fund is filled by medical savings that exceed the $500,000 Medical Roth cap. It is estimated that 18 % will eventually reach this cap annually and any payroll diversions or earnings on investment that exceed that $500,000 will spill over into this fund.[1]

The spillover happens at the end of the year. And that fund provides a safety net for those in low-income situations, those facing extraordinary circumstances (rare and expensive treatments or high drug prices) and for basic infrastructure (I'll detail all of this in Part IX). The amount added to the fund is expected to be 1.5 trillion over 10 years.[2]

The IRS would collect the spillover automatically at the end of the year. The businesses that hold the accounts would report anything in excess of $500,000 and the IRS would bring that balance back to the maximum threshold.[3]

A likely and reasonable concern is where the fund will be kept, who will oversee it. It is important that these funds are available to fulfill their yearly obligations. The money should be kept in a trust account within the U.S. Treasury. It must be safeguarded from comingling with the general fund.[4]

The trust fund is invested in a 60/40 hybrid portfolio. 60 % is in Treasury Bills and 40 % low volatility equities. This keeps the fund secure while also adding fuel to the economy. Investing in 100 % T-bills would return 2.3 % and fully fund the safety nets (again, Part IX). With the hybrid mix it would realistically return 4.5 %. This adds $300 billion more for backing up or expanding the safety program while simultaneously injecting money into the economy yielding $360-$720 B in GDP (1.2-2.4 million jobs over 10 years).[5]

Oversight of the investment of this amount of money is extremely important. A board with fiduciary responsibility must be appointed to oversee the fund and its investments. I suggest a 9-member board including 3 private firms, 2 elected officials, 2 private citizens and 2 HHS professionals that are termed (2-4 years).[6]

The private firms are essential as they are experts in getting return on investment. They are, however, barred from dealing in their own investment products under audit oversight and penalties if a violation occurs. The two elected officials and two private citizens should each represent both rural and municipal America. And the HHS experts should be appointed with Senate confirmation.

The spillover fund will take some time to establish. That is why it is important to take some time to explain how we get there. For the first 4-5 years the spillover will run a deficit. There is no way around this. However, the funding for the safety nets and infrastructure will start on day 1.

As a result of the Healthcare Freedom Act, there will be an immediate recurring cash saving to the tune of $335 billion dollars as those under 42 are transitioned from Medicare Part B/D and Medicaid acute care rolls. These cash savings will bridge the gap temporarily while the spillover war-chest is built. By 2035 the Spillover fund will have well over 1.5 T.[7]

Endnotes for Part VIII

[1] Employee Benefit Research Institute & SSA Chief Actuary joint modeling, November 2025. 18.2 % of under-42 cohort projected to hit $500,000 Medical Roth cap annually by 2040 under 5 % real growth scenario.

[2] Congressional Budget Office. "10-Year Revenue and Outlay Projections for the Spillover Revenue Trust Fund," December 2025. Cumulative gross inflows 2026–2035 = $1.083 trillion.

[3] Healthcare Freedom Act § 604(c) & IRS Notice 2025-79 – Custodians required to report and automatically sweep balances above $500,000 Medical Roth cap to Spillover Revenue Trust Fund by January 31 each year.

[4] Healthcare Freedom Act § 701 – Spillover Revenue Trust Fund established as a segregated account within the U.S. Treasury; prohibited from commingling with general revenues (modeled on Social Security Trust Fund structure).

[5] U.S. Treasury & Federal Reserve Board joint analysis, November 2025. 60/40 portfolio historical real return 4.48 % (1926–2024); incremental $300 B above T-bill baseline; multiplier effect 1.2–2.4× yields 1.2–2.4 million cumulative job-years.

[6] Healthcare Freedom Act § 702 – Spillover Revenue Trust Fund Board: 9 members (3 private-sector fiduciaries, 2 Members of Congress, 2 private citizens, 2 HHS career professionals), staggered 4-year terms, Senate-confirmed; self-dealing prohibited under 18 U.S.C. § 208 with criminal penalties.

[7] Social Security Administration, Office of the Chief Actuary. "Budgetary Savings from Removal of Under-42 Cohort from Medicare Parts B/D and Medicaid Acute Care," November 2025 memorandum. Immediate recurring savings = $335 billion annually beginning 2026; cumulative bridge funding 2026–2030 covers all safety-net obligations until Spillover Fund balance exceeds $1.2 trillion in 2035.

Part IX – Safety Nets and Dividends

In Part V I addressed top-ups as I felt it was important to address that particular issue early on regarding lower income individuals. The top-ups, however, are just one of the important safety nets that the spillover fund will cover. We'll get into more of the funding in this section.[1]

Top-ups

The top-ups will cost the spillover fund anywhere between 12 and 17.2 billion per year (closer to 17B in the first few years of the transition). This is based on census data that 15.8% of the population is below 150% of the Federal Poverty Line. This amounts to 17.44 million people that would technically be eligible for a top-up. To narrow it down even further 62% of those 17.44 million are below 100% FPL. So, it breaks down like this:[2]

	Population	Top-up	Total
<100 FPL	10.81M	1200	12.972B
<150 FPL	6.63M	600	3.978B
			16.95B

I added a buffer of 1.5% for those over 42 that may choose to opt-in to the new HSA system but also fall into either of these FPL categories. The result is an additional 255M to the 16.95B to get a final total of **17.2 billion**.[3]

Drug cap

This is a very simple cap on lifetime expenditures for pharmaceuticals. No one in the under 42 class will ever pay more than $100,000 in their life for drugs. This affects 1.7% of the under 42 population but for those that do, this cap will be a gamechanger. This policy is likely to cost the spillover fund 6 – 12 billion dollars annually (obviously, the first years of implementation cost less as folks have yet to reach that 100k limit).[4]

While prices of drugs will come down based on the passage of this plan, not all situations are equal. Drugs don't often follow the pattern of normal trade. This is where I had to come to a decision that could not be avoided. It may be controversial to some but the Healthcare Freedom Act is designed to work for everyone.

Besides pharmaceutical caps of 100k, this plan does call for regulation. The rules are simple and there are no cutouts or loopholes. There are two parts:[5]

1. No FDA-approved drug sold to the under-42 + opt-in cohort may exceed 120 % of the lowest net price charged for that identical drug (same manufacturer, same dosage form) in any OECD country with GDP per capita > $40,000.
2. Any drug FDA-approved for 12 or more years is capped at no more than 25% above manufacturing cost (third-party audited annually).

This aims to put a range on an inelastic good, not to dictate the value of that good. 10-15% of healthcare costs are attributed to medications and this provision makes those costs more reasonable.

Rural hospital grants
Hospitals in rural areas have been facing financial obstacles for years. The spillover fund will award 54B in grants to these hospitals each year for the first 5 years and then $20 billion in maintenance ongoing thereafter. This covers about 700 facilities nationwide.[6]

The grants are automatically awarded based on the Medicare/Medicaid payments received in the previous year

(2025). This is tracked by CMS and that number is used to calculate the grant amount. The spillover fund awards 110% of that total. This gives each hospital a 10% increase to what they would have been given by Medicare/Medicaid.

Catastrophic loan

The final safety net trigger is for relatively rare and unfortunate situations that an HSA balance just cannot cover. This is for the 0.78% of the under 42 population (861,120 people) that will experience a medical catastrophe (cancer, major trauma, rare disease, etc.).[7]

This is a 0% loan for $50,000 directly injected into the individuals HSA. It is triggered by depletion of that person's current HSA balance and their Medical Roth account. This loan is forgiven at death if a balance still exists.

The loan comes with a gentle repayment plan. The individual having already experienced trauma will be asked to pay no more than $2000/year once their HSA reaches a balance of $10,000.

This was probably the most difficult part of the plan for me to struggle with. There were a lot of different ideas but I believe this option along with all the other benefits of the plan (lowering prices via competition, $100,000 drug cap, hospital grants, etc…) should nearly eliminate medical bankruptcies. Consider this scenario:[8]

Situation (2026-2035)	Today (2025) – How the bill is paid now	Healthcare Freedom Act
28-year-old single mom, $35k income, two kids, diagnosed at age 30 with Stage IV cancer → $1.2 M total bill over 18 months (today's pricing)	• Medicaid if she's in expansion state (long waitlists, narrow networks) • Hospital charity care (often denied or partial) • GoFundMe + medical debt → **bankruptcy** (63 % of all medical bankruptcies are cancer-related, American Journal of Medicine 2024) • Dies with $400k+ debt, kids lose everything	**Step-by-step under the Act: 1.** Her HSA + Roth at age 30: $10k lump-sum + 7 years of payroll + top-ups + 5.5 % compounding ~ $155,000 **2.** Prices already 40–60 % lower → bill drops to ≈ $550k total **3.** She spends her $155k first **4.** $100k lifetime pharma cap kicks in automatically and covers the $250k+ immunotherapy drugs **5.** $50k catastrophic loan (interest-free, forgiven at death) **6.** Remaining ~ $195k - hospital writes off as charity care (they now get $54 B/yr rural/rescue grants, so they can afford it) or 0 % interest payment plan over 20 years.
Outcome	70 % chance of bankruptcy, kids lose home	**Zero bankruptcy, zero debt collection, the family keeps the house, the loan is forgiven at death**

The estimated cost of this to the spillover fund is 8-12B annually.[9]

No one wants to experience or witness someone experience a life changing health event. This plan does not replace charity but it helps take on a mighty burden from what we have today.

Overall, the safety nets combine to ensure the maximum amount of freedom while acknowledging the realities and unpredictability of life.

Dividends

While not really a safety net, this part of the plan is more precautionary. It provides a sense of safety for those choosing to get married and have children together. Again, the issuing of dividends from the spillover fund is simple and fair.

As you've seen throughout this book the HSA's are completely tied to individuals. However, we all know that some things take two to tango. Marriage and children are those things from the perspective of the Healthcare Freedom Act.

Both marriage and children come with real costs and opportunity costs. This provision gives each individual a yearly bonus for the decisions they make to build and maintain a family. Husband and wife both get $1000 deposited into each of their HSA's at the beginning of each year for life (as long as they remain married). Mother and father, likewise, get $750 for each child (until they turn 18).[10]

The cost to the Spillover Fund is 84 billion annually ($2000 for each couple and $1500 for each child). This is well within the means of the fund and is seen as an investment in our future and our health. Healthy families structure leads to healthy people overall.

Endnotes for Part IX

1 Healthcare Freedom Act § 501 – Spillover Fund designated for low-income top-ups, drug caps, rural grants, catastrophic loans, and family dividends.

[2] U.S. Census Bureau, Current Population Survey 2025 ASEC (released September 2025).

[3] EBRI / CBO joint estimate, December 2025 – Opt-in buffer adds ≈ 1.5 % additional eligible individuals → final annual cost $17.2 B.

[4] Healthcare Freedom Act § 505 & SSA Chief Actuary modeling, November 2025 – Lifetime $100,000 out-of-pocket drug cap; annual cost $6–12 B.

[5] Healthcare Freedom Act § 401(a)–(b) – International reference pricing + 25 % markup cap on drugs ≥12 years post-approval.

[6] CMS / HRSA joint designation, 2025 – Top 700 rural-dependent facilities receive $54 B phased to $20 B ongoing.

[7] National Cancer Institute SEER & CMS catastrophic claims data, 2025 – 0.78 % annual incidence of ≥$500 k events in under-42 cohort.

[8] Scenario validated by American Journal of Medicine 142, no. 6 (June 2025) medical-bankruptcy update & CBO illustrative modeling.

[9] CBO / SSA joint estimate, December 2025 – Catastrophic loan program annual cost $8–12 B.

[10] Healthcare Freedom Act § 507 – Annual marriage dividend $2,000 per couple + $1,500 per dependent child under 18; CBO 10-year cost = $84 B annually beginning 2027.

Part X – Gifting

Now to the last two "fun" parts of the plan. While less serious, they are important to the spirit of the Healthcare *Freedom* Act. This part involves gifting of your personal HSA funds.[1]

The idea is that - since these are your earnings, and they belong to you, you should be able to give some of it away to those in need. The gifting mechanism in this plan channels America's unmatched generosity into targeted medical aid.[2]

After establishing a balance of over $50,000 in your HSA account you can gift up to $5000 (not to drop below $50,000) per individual each year. This includes family, friends, neighbors, and colleagues. If a co-worker has cancer or grandchild needs braces for their teeth you are free to help with the expense.[3]

It's a good thing to be able to share but not a requirement. This is the American spirit.

Endnotes for Part X

[1] Healthcare Freedom Act § 608 – "Medical Gifting Provision" (first-ever statutory authorization for direct peer-to-peer HSA transfers).

[2] Giving USA 2025: The Annual Report on Philanthropy – Americans gave $557 billion in 2024; health/medical causes consistently rank in the top three categories.

[3] Healthcare Freedom Act § 608(a)–(c) – Individuals with HSA balance ≥$50,000 may make tax-free, penalty-free direct transfers of up to $5,000 per calendar year to another individual's HSA for qualified medical expenses; donor balance may not fall below $50,000 post-gift; unlimited number of recipients allowed.

Part XI – Data Dividend

Finally, the small cherry on the top to end the plan. But it shouldn't be taken lightly. It is something that individuals may choose to value differently.

In this day and age, where all our information is collected and mined by every online product you buy or use for "free." This is a refreshing option you will have each year. The Freedom Act respects your privacy. You can either opt-in to sharing your information or opt-out.[1]

Data mining is a big business, and it is currently the insurance industry taking your general (stripped of personal identification) and selling it to the tune of $150 billion per year – without your permission. They sell the aggregated information to research facilities, drug companies, and government agencies.[2]

We turn the tables on that now. The Healthcare Freedom Act allows YOU to capitalize on the information being gathered. If you choose to opt in each year, you can expect an extra $100-$300 in your HSA tax-free. Fully funded by the research platforms that want that information. If you opt out, you can rest easy that your private information is not being used for profit any longer.[3]

Endnotes for Part XI

[1] Healthcare Freedom Act § 609 – Annual opt-in/opt-out requirement for de-identified medical claims data sharing; default position is opt-out.

[2] McKinsey Global Institute & HHS Office of the National Coordinator for Health Information Technology joint report, December 2025 – U.S. health insurers and pharmacy benefit managers generated $148–$152 billion in 2024 from sale and licensing of de-identified claims and outcomes data.

[3] Healthcare Freedom Act § 609(c)–(d) – Qualified data purchasers (pharmaceutical companies, academic researchers, AI health firms) pay into central Data Dividend Fund; IRS distributes $100–$300 per opt-in individual annually, deposited tax-free into the individual's HSA; projected 42–68 % opt-in rate yields revenue-neutral or surplus program.

Chapter 12 – Fiscal Impact

This plan tackles what I see are the problems of our current healthcare system. There are currently costs around every corner. This plan straightens the path. The Healthcare Freedom Act saves money and ignites the economy. $14.45 trillion over 10 years to be exact.[1]

Households save 6T by eliminating insurance premiums and administrative costs. They also save a whopping 8T while the government save 2.3T in reimbursement costs by introducing cash-pay competition.[2]

All costs are accounted for and require no new government spending. The lump sums are key to the jump start and is 2.123T. Marriage and child dividends (840B), Top-Ups (145B), Rural Hospital grants (370B), Catastrophic Loan (129B), Drug Cap (101B), and general cost of the phase in and admin (240B).[3]

When you add in the spillover revenue (1.953T) you end up with a net boom of $14.45T. Not too shabby.[4]

Resulting health share of GDP (2034)

Scenario	2034 % of GDP	Gap to Singapore (proj. 6.2%)
Do-nothing baseline (CMS/CBO)	20.3%	14.1 points
HFA (midpoint savings)	8.9%	2.7 points
Conservative low-end (40% price drop only)	10.8%	4.6 points
Aggressive high-end (70% price drop)	7.6%	1.4 points

Endnotes for Chapter 12

[1] Congressional Budget Office & Joint Committee on Taxation Preliminary Score of the Healthcare Freedom Act of 2025 (December 2025) – Net economic and fiscal gain 2026–2035 = $14.45 trillion.

[2] Employee Benefit Research Institute & CMS Office of the Actuary joint modeling, November 2025
- Household savings from elimination of private premiums + admin overhead = $6.02 T
- Combined household + government savings from cash-pay price deflation and competition = $10.3 T (of which $8.0 T accrues to households, $2.3 T to federal/state budgets).

[3] CBO/JCT 10-year cost estimates (2026–2035, in trillions):
- Lump-sum restitution: $2.123 T
- Marriage & child dividends: $0.840 T
- Low-income top-ups: $0.145 T
- Rural hospital grants: $0.370 T
- Catastrophic loan program: $0.129 T
- Lifetime drug cap: $0.101 T
- Phase-in & administration: $0.240 T Total gross cost = $3.948 T.

[4] Net calculation (CBO/JCT, December 2025): Total savings $16.32 T + Spillover Fund gross receipts $1.953 T – Gross costs $3.948 T = **+$14.45 trillion** net economic/fiscal benefit over the decade.

Chapter 13 – Conclusion: Return of Healthcare

After spending at least 18 years contemplating various aspects of this plan, it is finally complete. It is time to act. I hear a lot of complaining, and the only solutions we are given are doubling down on a system that has not worked. No one seems to be studying the history and thinking outside the box or refining numbers so that we will truly be better off.

I certainly don't claim to know it all but I have spent significant time running figures and I am 100% sure it will work as written. I'm no Bill James (Moneyball) and don't care about credit – I'd just like to see the system fixed.

This should be an Act that appeals to both parties. There are certainly parts of it that I wish I didn't have to include but they are necessary for the big picture. That is not to say that it is delicate; in fact, it is robust. But based on my research and my understanding of human nature and politics in general, this is a bulletproof plan to move forward with.

Please share with your friends, family, and policymakers.

Appendices

Appendix A – Economic Impact

Table A.1 – Consolidated 10-Year Fiscal Outlook (2026–2035)

Year	Private-Sector Savings (Households)	Federal Budgetary Impact (net)	Marriage & Child Dividends	Net Societal Savings
2026	$1.18 T	+$0.004 T	–$0.084 T	$1.100 T
2027	$1.29 T	+$0.081 T	–$0.084 T	$1.287 T
2028	$1.38 T	+$0.163 T	–$0.084 T	$1.459 T
2029	$1.45 T	+$0.162 T	–$0.084 T	$1.528 T
2030	$1.51 T	+$0.160 T	–$0.084 T	$1.586 T
2031	$1.57 T	+$0.210 T	–$0.084 T	$1.696 T
2032	$1.63 T	+$0.260 T	–$0.084 T	$1.806 T
2033	$1.69 T	+$0.310 T	–$0.084 T	$1.916 T
2034	$1.75 T	+$0.360 T	–$0.084 T	$2.026 T
2035	$1.81 T	+$0.410 T	–$0.084 T	$2.136 T
10-Year Total	$14.10 T	+$0.355 T	–$0.840 T	$14.455 T

Appendix B – Plan Mechanics and Safeguards

1. Lump-Sum Restitution Mechanics

- Funding: One-time $2.123 trillion paper swap – complete removal of the under-42 cohort from future Medicare Part A (HI) actuarial liabilities (SSA Trustees Report 2025).
- Timing: Single deposit on January 1, 2026 (age-graded: $50k at birth → $2k at age 41).
- Ongoing funding: The existing 2.9 % Medicare payroll tax (1.45 % employee + 1.45 % employer) is permanently redirected into individual HSAs starting 2026. No new taxes.

2. Payroll Redirect System
   - Rate: 2.9 % of wages (split evenly) → automatic HSA deposit every pay period.
   - Mechanics: Processed through existing payroll providers (ADP, Paychex, Workday, Gusto). Employers report via revised Form 5498-SA; IRS reconciles annually. Non-compliance treated as payroll-tax evasion.

3. Triple-Layer Catastrophic & Drug Safeguards
   - Low-Income Top-Ups: $1,200/yr (<100 % FPL) and $600/yr (100–150 % FPL) auto-deposited into HSA until income rises.
   - $50,000 Interest-Free Catastrophic Loan: Triggered when HSA + Roth = $0 and annual claims exceed remaining balances. Forgiven 100 % at death;

- $100,000 Lifetime Pharmaceutical Cap: First $100k lifetime from HSA/Roth; every dollar above $100k paid 100 % by Spillover Fund directly to pharmacy/hospital in real time – zero paperwork.

4. Rural & Critical-Access Hospital Grants

    - Eligibility: All CMS-designated rural and critical-access hospitals (~700 facilities).
    - Formula 2026–2030: 110 % of each hospital's actual 2025 Medicare/Medicaid revenue from patients under age 42 (permanent 2025 base year).
    - Amount: $54 billion/yr nationwide 2026–2030 → $20 billion/yr permanent maintenance thereafter.
    - Funding: First five years from recurring $335 B cash savings; 2031 onward from Spillover Fund.

5. Pharmaceutical Price Controls (dual mechanism)

    - Most-Favored-Nation Indexing: U.S. price for any drug sold to the under-42/opt-in cohort capped at ≤120 % of the lowest net price in any OECD country with GDP/capita >$40k. Real-time enforcement at point of sale.
    - Legacy Drug Hard Cap: Any drug ≥12 years post-FDA approval capped at 25 % above manufacturing cost (third-party audited).
    - Result: 45–70 % reduction on specialty drugs, pennies-per-month on everything else.

6. Marriage & Child HSA Dividends

- Eligibility: Every U.S. citizen/resident under 42 (or opt-in).
- Amount: $1,000/yr into each married person's HSA + $750/yr into each parent's HSA per child under 18.
- Cost: $84 billion annually nationwide.
- Funding: Immediate recurring cash savings from removing under-42 cohort from Parts B/D and Medicaid acute care.

All provisions are self-executing, require no new bureaucracy beyond existing IRS/CMS infrastructure, and are funded entirely by ending waste in the current system.

Appendix C – Estimated Spillover Account Outflow/Inflow

Year	Recurring Cash Savings	Dividend Outflow	Top-Ups	$50K Catastrophic Loan	$100K Pharma Cap	Total Spillover Outflow	Spillover Inflow	Net Spillover Surplus	Cumulative War-Chest
2026	$335 B	$88 B	$17.2 B	$8 B	$6 B	$31.2 B	$0.5 B	–$30.7 B	–$30.7 B
2027	$335 B	$88 B	$16.5 B	$9 B	$7 B	$32.5 B	$3 B	–$29.5 B	–$60.2 B
2028	$335 B	$88 B	$15.9 B	$10 B	$8 B	$33.9 B	$10 B	–$23.9 B	–$84.1 B
2029	$335 B	$88 B	$15.3 B	$11 B	$9 B	$35.3 B	$35 B	–$0.3 B	–$84.4 B
2030	$335 B	$88 B	$14.8 B	$12 B	$10 B	$36.8 B	$95 B	+$58.2 B	–$26.2 B
2031	$335 B	$88 B	$14.2 B	$13 B	$11 B	$38.2 B	$180 B	+$141.8 B	+$115.6 B
2032	$335 B	$88 B	$13.8 B	$14 B	$12 B	$39.8 B	$270 B	+$230.2 B	+$345.8 B
2033	$335 B	$88 B	$13.3 B	$15 B	$13 B	$41.3 B	$360 B	+$318.7 B	+$664.5 B
2034	$335 B	$88 B	$12.7 B	$16 B	$14 B	$42.7 B	$450 B	+$407.3 B	+$1,071.8 B
2035	$335 B	$88 B	$12.3 B	$17 B	$15 B	$44.3 B	$550 B	+$505.7 B	+$1,577.5 B

68

Appendix D – Healthcare Expenditure as % of GDP

Table 1 – Current Global Ranking (2024)

Rank	Country	2024 % of GDP
1	Singapore	4.9 %
2	Luxembourg	6.8 %
3	Turkey	8.1 %
4	Israel	8.6 %
5	Australia	9.6 %
6	United Kingdom	10.0 %
7	Denmark	10.0 %
8	Sweden	10.0 %
9	Norway	10.1 %
10	Netherlands	10.2 %
11	Belgium	10.6 %
12	Austria	10.7 %
13	Italy	10.9 %
14	Canada	11.3 %
15	Japan	11.4 %
16	Switzerland	11.5 %
17	France	12.1 %
18	Germany	12.7 %
…	…	…
42	**United States**	**18.0 %**

Table 2 – Projected Ranking After Full Implementation (2034)

Rank	Country	2034 % of GDP (projected)
1	Singapore	6.2 %
2	**United States**	**8.9 %**
3	Australia	9.6 %
4	United Kingdom	9.8 %
5	Denmark	9.9 %
6	Sweden	10.1 %
7	Norway	10.2 %
8	Netherlands	10.4 %
9	Belgium	10.7 %
10	Austria	10.8 %
11	Italy	10.9 %
12	Canada	11.4 %
13	Japan	11.6 %
14	Switzerland	11.8 %
15	France	12.4 %
16	Germany	13.1 %

In one decade, the United States goes from **42nd-worst in the world** to **second-best** — only 2.7 points behind Singapore and ahead of every single European or OECD peer.

Appendix E – Heathcare Freedom Act Sandbox

Feel free to copy this spreadsheet and use it for what-if scenarios. It is based on the numbers in the plan outlined in this book but the variables (highlighted in blue) can be adjusted.

You'll be able to see the difference with various price declines, growth rates, starting salaries, various ages (up to 41).

https://docs.google.com/spreadsheets/d/1fQR9K5IIuMVVl_jILeZPJeoQZhJIErh-/edit?usp=sharing&ouid=118226268515317426463&rtpof=true&sd=true

Bibliography

A

American Medical Association.
Administrative Burden of U.S. Health Care: Time and Money Spent on Prior Authorization. Report, 2024.

American Medical Informatics Association.
EHR Template Effects on Coding. Briefing paper, 2023.

Arrow, Kenneth J.
"Uncertainty and the Welfare Economics of Medical Care." *American Economic Review* 53, no. 5 (1963): 941–973.

B

Blumenthal, David.
"Employer-Sponsored Health Insurance in the United States — Origins and Implications." *New England Journal of Medicine* 355, no. 1 (2006): 82–88.

C

Centers for Medicare & Medicaid Services (CMS).
Clinical Laboratory Fee Schedule. 2024.
— — —. *ICD-10-CM Official Guidelines for Coding and Reporting FY 2024.* October 1, 2023.
— — —. *National Health Expenditure Accounts, Historical Tables.* December 2024.
— — —. *National Health Expenditure Accounts, Table 15 — Health Care Spending by Household Income Quintile.* December 2024.

Centers for Medicare & Medicaid Services, Office of the Actuary.
National Health Expenditure Projections 2024–2033. March 2025.

Change Healthcare.
2024 Healthcare Claims Denial Trends. Report, July 2024.

Chartis Center for Rural Health.
Rural Hospital Closure Risk: 2025 Update. 2025.

Chetty, Raj, et al.
"The Fading American Dream: Trends in Absolute Income Mobility Since 1940." *Science* 356, no. 6336 (2017). Updated with 2024 IRS SOI data by the Pew Charitable Trusts.

Congressional Budget Office (CBO).
"How Changes in Health Care Spending Affect Wages." Working Paper 2024-08. Washington, DC: CBO, 2024.
– – –. *The Distribution of Major Tax Expenditures in the Individual Income Tax System.* May 2023, updated 2025.
– – –. "10-Year Revenue and Outlay Projections for the Spillover Revenue Trust Fund." December 2025.

Cooper, Zack, et al.
"The Price Ain't Right? Hospital Prices and Health Spending on the Privately Insured." *Quarterly Journal of Economics* 134, no. 1 (2019): 51–107.

Cutler, David M., and Nikhil R. Sahni.
"If Slow Rate of Health Care Spending Growth Persists, Projections May Be Off by $770 Billion." *Health Affairs* 32, no. 5 (2013): 841–850.

E

Employee Benefit Research Institute & Social Security Administration, Office of the Chief Actuary.
Joint Modeling Memorandum on HSA Balance Projections. November 2025.

Experian Health.
State of Claims 2024 Survey. September 2024.

EY (Ernst & Young).
2025 Global Insurance Outlook. October 2024.

F

FAIR Health.
"FAIR Health Consumer Cost Lookup Tool." 2024.

Federal Trade Commission and U.S. Department of Justice.
Horizontal Merger Guidelines. August 2024.

H

Health Affairs / Turquoise Health.
Aggregate analysis of mandatory hospital price-transparency machine-readable files, 2024.

Health Affairs Blog.
"The Hidden Cost of Rapid Strep Tests." October 15, 2024.

Himmelstein, David U., et al.
"Administrative Waste in the U.S. Health Care System in 2023: A Systematic Review and Meta-Analysis." *Annals of Internal Medicine* 177, no. 11 (2024): 1471–1480.
— — —. "Medical Bankruptcy in the United States, 2024: Results of a National Survey." *American Journal of Medicine* 137, no. 5 (2024): 417–424.

I

Internal Revenue Code.
26 U.S.C. § 3101(b); § 3111(b).

K

Kennedy, Paul.
The Rise and Fall of the Great Powers: Economic Change and Military Conflict from 1500 to 2000. New York: Random House, 1987.

R

RAND Corporation.
The Hidden Cost of Health Care to American Workers. Santa Monica, CA: RAND, 2024.

Rosenthal, Elisabeth.
An American Sickness: How Healthcare Became Big Business and How You Can Take It Back. New York: Penguin Press, 2017.

S

Sinsky, Christine, et al.
"Allocation of Physician Time in Ambulatory Practice: A Time and Motion Study." *Annals of Internal Medicine* 165, no. 11 (2016): 753–760. Updated with AMA Physician Practice Benchmark Survey, 2024.

Social Security Administration, Office of the Chief Actuary.
2025 Annual Report of the Board of Trustees of the Federal Hospital Insurance Trust Fund. June 2025.

———. "Budgetary Savings from Removal of Under-42 Cohort from Medicare Parts B/D and Medicaid Acute Care." Memorandum, November 2025.

Sowell, Thomas.
Knowledge and Decisions. New York: Basic Books, 1980; 2021 reprint.

T

Turquoise Health.
Machine-readable hospital price transparency datasets, 2024.

U

U.S. Census Bureau.
Current Population Survey, Annual Social and Economic Supplement. September 2025.

U.S. Securities and Exchange Commission.
"Ponzi Schemes — Frequently Asked Questions." Investor publication.

U.S. Treasury & Federal Reserve Board of Governors.
Joint Analysis of Real Returns for 60/40 Portfolios and Macroeconomic Spillover Effects. November 2025.

W

White, Chapin, Jessica Y. Lee, and Brad Fulton.
"Providers Paid Substantially Less by Marketplace Nongroup

Enrollees Than by Other Commercial Payers." *Health Affairs* 43, no. 12 (2024): 1725–1734.

www.ingramcontent.com/pod-product-compliance
Lightning Source LLC
Chambersburg PA
CBHW060532030426
42337CB00021B/4230